50 Air Fryer Adventure Recipes for Home

By: Kelly Johnson

Table of Contents

- Classic Air Fryer Chicken Wings
- Crispy Air Fried French Fries
- Garlic Parmesan Air Fryer Brussels Sprouts
- Lemon Pepper Air Fryer Salmon
- Air Fried Chicken Tenders
- Air Fryer Sweet Potato Fries
- Buffalo Cauliflower Bites
- Air Fryer Shrimp Scampi
- Teriyaki Chicken Skewers
- BBQ Pulled Pork Sliders
- Crispy Air Fryer Mozzarella Sticks
- Coconut Shrimp with Mango Salsa
- Air Fried Avocado Fries
- Eggplant Parmesan Bites
- Jalapeño Poppers
- Air Fryer Zucchini Chips
- Ranch Chicken Tenders
- Honey Mustard Glazed Salmon
- Parmesan Crusted Air Fryer Chicken Breast
- Cinnamon Sugar Air Fryer Donuts
- Spicy Sweet Potato Wedges
- Asian-Inspired Sesame Chicken
- Southwest Egg Rolls
- Caprese Stuffed Portobello Mushrooms
- Bacon-Wrapped Jalapeño Poppers
- Air Fryer Teriyaki Tofu
- Garlic Herb Air Fryer Pork Chops
- Mediterranean Stuffed Peppers
- Crispy Coconut Chicken Strips
- Air Fryer Shrimp Tacos
- Lemon Garlic Butter Shrimp
- Sweet and Spicy Chicken Drumsticks
- Pesto Zoodle (Zucchini Noodle) Bowl
- Air Fried Pickles
- Apple Cinnamon Air Fryer Pancakes

- Blackened Salmon Tacos
- Cheesy Broccoli Bites
- Maple Glazed Bacon-Wrapped Dates
- Coconut Crusted Tilapia
- Air Fryer Corn on the Cob
- Chicken Parmesan Meatballs
- Cajun Sweet Potato Fries
- Mediterranean Chickpea Salad
- Teriyaki Pineapple Chicken Skewers
- Rosemary Garlic Roasted Potatoes
- Air Fryer Ratatouille
- Chocolate Chip Banana Bread Muffins
- Pecan-Crusted Air Fryer Chicken Tenders
- Lemon Herb Roasted Asparagus
- Air Fryer Beef and Vegetable Kebabs

Classic Air Fryer Chicken Wings

Ingredients:

Chicken wings (split into flats and drumettes)
Salt and pepper to taste
Garlic powder
Onion powder
Paprika
Baking powder (optional, for extra crispiness)
Olive oil or cooking spray

Instructions:

Preheat the Air Fryer:

Preheat your air fryer to 400°F (200°C).
Prepare the Chicken Wings:
- Pat the chicken wings dry with paper towels to remove excess moisture.
- In a large bowl, season the wings with salt, pepper, garlic powder, onion powder, and paprika. Adjust the quantities to your taste preferences.

Optional: Use Baking Powder:
- If you want extra crispiness, you can add a tablespoon of baking powder to the seasoning mixture. This helps achieve a crispy exterior.

Coat with Olive Oil:
- Lightly coat the seasoned wings with olive oil or use a cooking spray. This helps them become golden brown and crispy during the air frying process.

Arrange in the Air Fryer Basket:
- Place the wings in a single layer in the air fryer basket, ensuring they are not overcrowded. You may need to cook in batches if your air fryer has limited space.

Air Fry:
- Cook the wings in the preheated air fryer for about 25-30 minutes, flipping them halfway through the cooking time. Adjust the time based on the size and thickness of the wings, ensuring they reach an internal temperature of 165°F (74°C).

Check for Crispiness:
- Open the air fryer and check the wings for crispiness. If needed, cook for an additional 5 minutes for extra crispiness.

Serve:
- Once the wings are cooked to perfection, transfer them to a serving plate. You can serve them as is or with your favorite dipping sauces.

Enjoy:
- Serve the classic air fryer chicken wings hot, and enjoy them as a delicious appetizer or party snack.

These air-fried chicken wings are a crowd-pleaser, offering a perfect balance of crispy skin and succulent meat. Feel free to customize the seasoning and sauces to suit your taste preferences.

Crispy Air Fried French Fries

Ingredients:

    Potatoes (russet or your preferred variety)
    Olive oil
    Salt and pepper to taste
    Optional: Garlic powder, onion powder, paprika, or other seasonings

Instructions:

Preheat the Air Fryer:
- Preheat your air fryer to 380°F (193°C).

Prepare the Potatoes:
- Wash and peel the potatoes if desired. Cut them into evenly sized matchsticks or wedges.

Soak in Water (Optional):
- If you have time, soak the cut potatoes in cold water for about 30 minutes. This helps remove excess starch and makes the fries crispier. Pat the potatoes dry with a clean kitchen towel afterward.

Season the Fries:
- In a bowl, toss the potato sticks with olive oil, salt, pepper, and any optional seasonings like garlic powder, onion powder, or paprika. Ensure the fries are evenly coated.

Arrange in the Air Fryer Basket:
- Place the seasoned fries in the air fryer basket in a single layer, making sure not to overcrowd. You may need to cook in batches for best results.

Air Fry:
- Cook the fries in the preheated air fryer for 20-25 minutes, shaking or flipping them halfway through to ensure even cooking. Adjust the time based on the thickness of the fries and your desired level of crispiness.

Check for Crispiness:
- Open the air fryer and check the fries for doneness. If needed, cook for an additional 5 minutes for extra crispiness.

Serve:
- Once the fries are golden brown and crispy, transfer them to a serving plate. Season with additional salt if necessary.

Enjoy:

- Serve the crispy air-fried French fries hot, and enjoy them with your favorite dipping sauces or condiments.

These air-fried French fries are a healthier alternative to traditional deep-fried ones, and they still deliver a satisfying crunch. Feel free to experiment with different seasonings and dipping sauces to suit your taste preferences.

Garlic Parmesan Air Fryer Brussels Sprouts

Ingredients:

    Brussels sprouts, trimmed and halved
    Olive oil
    Garlic powder
    Parmesan cheese, grated
    Salt and pepper to taste
    Optional: Red pepper flakes for a hint of spice

Instructions:

    Preheat the Air Fryer:
- Preheat your air fryer to 375°F (190°C).

    Prepare the Brussels Sprouts:
- Trim the ends of the Brussels sprouts and cut them in half. If they are large, you can quarter them for more even cooking.

    Season the Brussels Sprouts:
- In a bowl, toss the halved Brussels sprouts with olive oil until evenly coated. Add garlic powder, grated Parmesan cheese, salt, pepper, and red pepper flakes (if using). Mix well to ensure the Brussels sprouts are evenly seasoned.

    Arrange in the Air Fryer Basket:
- Place the seasoned Brussels sprouts in the air fryer basket, spreading them out to ensure they cook evenly.

    Air Fry:
- Cook the Brussels sprouts in the preheated air fryer for 12-15 minutes, shaking or tossing them halfway through to promote even cooking. Adjust the time based on the size of the Brussels sprouts and your desired level of crispiness.

    Check for Crispiness:
- Open the air fryer and check the Brussels sprouts for crispiness. Continue cooking for an additional 3-5 minutes if needed.

    Serve:
- Once the Brussels sprouts are golden brown and crispy, transfer them to a serving dish.

    Finish with Parmesan:

- Sprinkle additional grated Parmesan cheese over the top while the Brussels sprouts are still warm.

Enjoy:
- Serve the Garlic Parmesan Air Fryer Brussels Sprouts hot as a delicious and flavorful side dish.

These air-fried Brussels sprouts are crispy on the outside, tender on the inside, and loaded with the savory flavors of garlic and Parmesan. They make a fantastic addition to any meal or a tasty snack.

Lemon Pepper Air Fryer Salmon

Ingredients:

- Salmon fillets
- Olive oil
- Lemon zest
- Lemon juice
- Black pepper, freshly ground
- Salt to taste
- Garlic powder (optional)
- Fresh parsley, chopped (for garnish)

Instructions:

Preheat the Air Fryer:
- Preheat your air fryer to 375°F (190°C).

Prepare the Salmon:
- Pat the salmon fillets dry with paper towels to remove excess moisture.
- Drizzle the fillets with olive oil, ensuring they are lightly coated.

Season the Salmon:
- Sprinkle lemon zest and freshly ground black pepper over the salmon fillets. Add salt to taste. Optionally, you can add a touch of garlic powder for extra flavor.

Squeeze Lemon Juice:
- Drizzle fresh lemon juice over the seasoned salmon fillets. This adds a bright and citrusy flavor to the dish.

Arrange in the Air Fryer Basket:
- Place the seasoned salmon fillets in the air fryer basket, ensuring they are not crowded. You may need to cook in batches if your air fryer has limited space.

Air Fry:
- Cook the salmon in the preheated air fryer for 10-12 minutes, depending on the thickness of the fillets. Check for doneness by flaking the salmon with a fork. It should easily flake and be opaque in the center.

Garnish:
- Sprinkle freshly chopped parsley over the cooked salmon for a burst of freshness.

Serve:

- Carefully remove the Lemon Pepper Air Fryer Salmon from the basket and transfer it to a serving plate.

Enjoy:
- Serve the salmon hot, and enjoy this flavorful and healthy dish.

This Lemon Pepper Air Fryer Salmon is not only quick and easy to make but also full of zesty and savory flavors. It's a great option for a weeknight dinner or a light and nutritious meal.

Air Fried Chicken Tenders

Ingredients:

- 1 pound chicken tenders
- 1 cup buttermilk
- 1 cup all-purpose flour
- 1 teaspoon garlic powder
- 1 teaspoon onion powder
- 1 teaspoon paprika
- 1/2 teaspoon salt
- 1/4 teaspoon black pepper
- Cooking spray or oil for misting

Instructions:

Marinate the Chicken:
- Place the chicken tenders in a bowl and pour the buttermilk over them.
- Allow the chicken to marinate in the buttermilk for at least 30 minutes or overnight in the refrigerator. This helps tenderize the chicken and adds flavor.

Prepare the Coating:
- In a shallow dish, combine the flour, garlic powder, onion powder, paprika, salt, and black pepper. Mix well to ensure even seasoning.

Coat the Chicken:
- Preheat your air fryer to 400°F (200°C).
- Remove the chicken tenders from the buttermilk, allowing any excess to drip off.
- Dredge each tender in the flour mixture, ensuring an even coating. Press the flour mixture onto the chicken to help it adhere.

Air Frying:
- Lightly coat the air fryer basket with cooking spray or brush with oil.
- Place the coated chicken tenders in a single layer in the air fryer basket, ensuring they are not overcrowded.
- Lightly mist the top of the chicken tenders with cooking spray.

Cooking:
- Air fry the chicken tenders at 400°F (200°C) for 12-15 minutes, flipping halfway through the cooking time.

- Cooking times may vary depending on the thickness of the chicken tenders and the specific model of your air fryer. Ensure the internal temperature reaches 165°F (74°C).

Serve:
- Once the chicken tenders are golden brown and cooked through, remove them from the air fryer.
- Allow them to rest for a few minutes before serving.

Optional Dipping Sauce:
- Serve with your favorite dipping sauce, such as honey mustard, barbecue sauce, or ranch.

Enjoy your crispy and flavorful air-fried chicken tenders!

Air Fryer Sweet Potato Fries

Ingredients:

- 2 large sweet potatoes, peeled and cut into fries
- 2 tablespoons olive oil
- 1 teaspoon paprika
- 1/2 teaspoon garlic powder
- 1/2 teaspoon onion powder
- 1/2 teaspoon cayenne pepper (adjust to taste)
- 1/2 teaspoon salt (or to taste)
- 1/4 teaspoon black pepper
- Cooking spray

Instructions:

Preparation:
- Preheat your air fryer to 400°F (200°C).

Cut the Sweet Potatoes:
- Peel the sweet potatoes and cut them into evenly sized fries. Try to make the fries as uniform as possible for even cooking.

Coat with Olive Oil and Seasoning:
- In a large bowl, toss the sweet potato fries with olive oil, paprika, garlic powder, onion powder, cayenne pepper, salt, and black pepper. Ensure that the fries are evenly coated with the seasoning.

Arrange in the Air Fryer:
- Lightly coat the air fryer basket with cooking spray.
- Place the seasoned sweet potato fries in the air fryer basket in a single layer, ensuring they are not overcrowded. You may need to cook in batches.

Air Frying:
- Cook the sweet potato fries at 400°F (200°C) for 15-20 minutes, shaking the basket halfway through to ensure even cooking.
- Cooking times may vary based on your specific air fryer and the thickness of the sweet potato fries. Aim for crispy and golden-brown fries.

Serve:
- Once the sweet potato fries are done, remove them from the air fryer.
- Allow them to cool for a few minutes before serving.

Optional Dipping Sauce:
- Serve with your favorite dipping sauce, such as aioli, ketchup, or a yogurt-based sauce.

Enjoy your delicious and crispy air-fried sweet potato fries as a tasty side or snack!

Buffalo Cauliflower Bites

Ingredients:

- 1 head of cauliflower, cut into bite-sized florets
- 1 cup all-purpose flour
- 1 cup water
- 1 teaspoon garlic powder
- 1 teaspoon onion powder
- 1/2 teaspoon paprika
- 1/4 teaspoon salt
- 1/4 teaspoon black pepper
- 1 cup buffalo sauce (store-bought or homemade)
- 2 tablespoons unsalted butter, melted
- Optional: Celery sticks and ranch or blue cheese dressing for serving

Instructions:

Preheat the Oven:
- Preheat your oven to 450°F (230°C).

Prepare the Cauliflower:
- Cut the cauliflower into bite-sized florets, discarding the tough stem.

Batter Mixture:
- In a bowl, whisk together the flour, water, garlic powder, onion powder, paprika, salt, and black pepper until you have a smooth batter.

Coat the Cauliflower:
- Dip each cauliflower floret into the batter, ensuring it's well-coated. Allow any excess batter to drip off.

Bake:
- Place the coated cauliflower on a baking sheet lined with parchment paper or a silicone baking mat.
- Bake in the preheated oven for 20-25 minutes or until the cauliflower is golden brown and crispy.

Prepare the Buffalo Sauce:
- While the cauliflower is baking, mix the buffalo sauce and melted butter in a bowl. Adjust the ratio to your desired level of spiciness.

Coat the Baked Cauliflower:
- Once the cauliflower is done baking, transfer it to a large bowl.
- Pour the buffalo sauce mixture over the baked cauliflower and toss until the cauliflower is evenly coated.

Serve:
- Serve the buffalo cauliflower bites hot, optionally with celery sticks and your favorite dipping sauce like ranch or blue cheese.

Enjoy your flavorful and spicy buffalo cauliflower bites as a tasty appetizer or snack!

Air Fryer Shrimp Scampi

Ingredients:

- 1 pound large shrimp, peeled and deveined
- 3 tablespoons olive oil
- 4 cloves garlic, minced
- 1/2 cup dry white wine
- Juice of 1 lemon
- Zest of 1 lemon
- 1/4 teaspoon red pepper flakes (optional, for some heat)
- Salt and black pepper to taste
- 2 tablespoons chopped fresh parsley
- 1 tablespoon grated Parmesan cheese (optional)
- Lemon wedges for serving

Instructions:

Preheat the Air Fryer:
- Preheat your air fryer to 400°F (200°C).

Prepare the Shrimp:
- In a bowl, toss the peeled and deveined shrimp with 1 tablespoon of olive oil, salt, and black pepper.

Air Fry the Shrimp:
- Place the seasoned shrimp in the air fryer basket in a single layer. Cook for 5-7 minutes, shaking the basket halfway through to ensure even cooking. The shrimp should be opaque and cooked through.

Prepare the Scampi Sauce:
- While the shrimp are cooking, heat the remaining 2 tablespoons of olive oil in a skillet over medium heat.
- Add minced garlic and sauté for about 1-2 minutes until fragrant but not browned.
- Pour in the white wine, lemon juice, lemon zest, and red pepper flakes (if using). Simmer for 2-3 minutes, allowing the flavors to meld.

Combine Shrimp and Scampi Sauce:
- Once the shrimp are done in the air fryer, transfer them to the skillet with the scampi sauce. Toss the shrimp in the sauce to coat them evenly.

Serve:
- Plate the shrimp scampi, garnish with chopped fresh parsley and grated Parmesan cheese if desired.

- Serve with lemon wedges on the side for an extra burst of citrus flavor.

Enjoy your air-fried shrimp scampi as a delicious and quick seafood dish!

Teriyaki Chicken Skewers

Ingredients:

For the Teriyaki Marinade:

- 1/2 cup soy sauce
- 1/4 cup water
- 3 tablespoons honey
- 2 tablespoons rice vinegar
- 1 tablespoon mirin (Japanese sweet rice wine)
- 1 tablespoon sesame oil
- 2 cloves garlic, minced
- 1 teaspoon ginger, grated
- 1 tablespoon cornstarch (optional, for thickening)

For the Chicken Skewers:

- 1.5 to 2 pounds boneless, skinless chicken thighs or chicken breast, cut into bite-sized pieces
- Wooden skewers, soaked in water for 30 minutes (if grilling)
- Sesame seeds and chopped green onions for garnish (optional)

Instructions:

Prepare the Marinade:
- In a bowl, whisk together soy sauce, water, honey, rice vinegar, mirin, sesame oil, minced garlic, and grated ginger. If you prefer a thicker sauce, you can add cornstarch to the marinade.

Marinate the Chicken:
- Place the chicken pieces in a shallow dish or a Ziploc bag.
- Pour half of the teriyaki marinade over the chicken, reserving the other half for basting and serving later.
- Marinate the chicken for at least 30 minutes to an hour in the refrigerator. For more flavor, you can marinate it longer or even overnight.

Skewering the Chicken:
- If grilling, thread the marinated chicken pieces onto the soaked wooden skewers.

Grill or Bake:
- Grill the skewers over medium-high heat for about 8-10 minutes, turning occasionally, until the chicken is cooked through and has a nice char.

- If baking, preheat your oven to 400°F (200°C). Place the skewers on a baking sheet lined with parchment paper and bake for 20-25 minutes or until the chicken is cooked through.

Basting:
- During the last few minutes of grilling or baking, baste the chicken with the reserved teriyaki marinade.

Serve:
- Garnish the teriyaki chicken skewers with sesame seeds and chopped green onions, if desired.
- Serve with extra teriyaki sauce on the side for dipping.

Enjoy these delicious teriyaki chicken skewers as a main course or as part of a flavorful Asian-inspired meal!

BBQ Pulled Pork Sliders

Ingredients:

For the Pulled Pork:

- 3-4 pounds pork shoulder or pork butt
- 1 tablespoon olive oil
- 1 onion, finely chopped
- 3 cloves garlic, minced
- 1 cup barbecue sauce (plus extra for serving)
- 1/2 cup chicken or vegetable broth
- 1 teaspoon smoked paprika
- 1 teaspoon cumin
- Salt and pepper to taste

For the Sliders:

- Slider buns
- Coleslaw (optional, for topping)
- Pickles (optional, for serving)

Instructions:

For the Pulled Pork:

    Prepare the Pork:
- Trim excess fat from the pork shoulder or pork butt. Season with salt and pepper.

    Sear the Pork:
- Heat olive oil in a large skillet or Dutch oven over medium-high heat. Sear the pork on all sides until browned.

    Saute Onions and Garlic:
- Add chopped onions and minced garlic to the skillet. Saute until the onions are softened.

    Combine Ingredients:
- Transfer the seared pork, sauteed onions, and garlic to a slow cooker. Add barbecue sauce, chicken or vegetable broth, smoked paprika, and cumin.

    Slow Cook:
- Cook on low for 6-8 hours or until the pork is tender and easily shreds with a fork.

    Shred the Pork:

- Once cooked, remove the pork from the slow cooker and shred it using two forks. Mix the shredded pork with the cooking juices and additional barbecue sauce if needed.

Assemble the Sliders:

Prepare the Buns:
- Slice the slider buns in half and lightly toast them in the oven or on a grill.

Assemble:
- Place a generous portion of the BBQ pulled pork on the bottom half of each slider bun.

Add Toppings:
- Top the pulled pork with coleslaw if desired, and add pickles for extra flavor.

Serve:
- Place the top half of the slider buns on the pulled pork to complete the sliders.

Enjoy your BBQ pulled pork sliders with your favorite sides and condiments! They make a delicious and satisfying meal for any occasion.

Crispy Air Fryer Mozzarella Sticks

Ingredients:

- 12 mozzarella sticks, cut in half (24 pieces)
- 1 cup all-purpose flour
- 2 large eggs, beaten
- 1 cup Italian-style breadcrumbs
- 1/2 cup grated Parmesan cheese
- 1 teaspoon dried oregano
- 1 teaspoon garlic powder
- 1/2 teaspoon onion powder
- Marinara sauce for dipping

Instructions:

Preheat the Air Fryer:
- Preheat your air fryer to 390°F (200°C).

Prepare the Breading Station:
- Set up a breading station with three shallow dishes. Place the flour in the first dish, beaten eggs in the second dish, and a mixture of breadcrumbs, Parmesan cheese, oregano, garlic powder, and onion powder in the third dish.

Coat Mozzarella Sticks:
- Take each mozzarella stick half and coat it in the flour, shaking off any excess.
- Dip the floured mozzarella stick into the beaten eggs, ensuring it is fully coated.
- Roll the mozzarella stick in the breadcrumb mixture, pressing the breadcrumbs onto the surface to adhere.

Repeat Breading:
- Repeat the process to double-coat the mozzarella sticks for extra crispiness. Dip each stick back into the beaten eggs and then into the breadcrumb mixture again.

Arrange in the Air Fryer:
- Place the breaded mozzarella sticks in a single layer in the air fryer basket, ensuring they are not touching.

Air Fry:

- Air fry the mozzarella sticks at 390°F (200°C) for 6-8 minutes or until they are golden brown and crispy. Cooking times may vary depending on the brand and model of your air fryer, so keep an eye on them.

Serve:
- Carefully remove the mozzarella sticks from the air fryer and let them cool for a minute.
- Serve the crispy mozzarella sticks with marinara sauce for dipping.

Enjoy your homemade crispy air fryer mozzarella sticks as a delightful and cheesy snack!

Coconut Shrimp with Mango Salsa

Ingredients:

For the Coconut Shrimp:

- 1 pound large shrimp, peeled and deveined
- 1 cup shredded coconut (unsweetened)
- 1 cup panko breadcrumbs
- 2 eggs, beaten
- 1/2 cup all-purpose flour
- Salt and black pepper to taste
- Cooking spray or oil for misting

For the Mango Salsa:

- 1 ripe mango, diced
- 1/2 red onion, finely chopped
- 1 red bell pepper, diced
- 1/4 cup fresh cilantro, chopped
- Juice of 1 lime
- Salt and pepper to taste

For Dipping Sauce (Optional):

- 1/2 cup sweet chili sauce
- 1 tablespoon soy sauce
- 1 teaspoon lime juice

Instructions:

For the Coconut Shrimp:

- Preheat the Oven:
    - Preheat your oven to 425°F (220°C).
- Prepare Breading Station:
    - Set up a breading station with three shallow dishes. Place flour in the first dish, beaten eggs in the second, and a mixture of shredded coconut and panko breadcrumbs in the third.
- Coat the Shrimp:
    - Season the shrimp with salt and black pepper.

- Dredge each shrimp in the flour, dip into the beaten eggs, and coat with the coconut-panko mixture, pressing the coating onto the shrimp to adhere.

Arrange on Baking Sheet:
- Place the breaded shrimp on a baking sheet lined with parchment paper or a silicone mat. Lightly mist the shrimp with cooking spray or brush with oil.

Bake:
- Bake in the preheated oven for 12-15 minutes or until the shrimp are golden brown and cooked through, flipping halfway through for even browning.

For the Mango Salsa:

Prepare Mango Salsa:
- In a bowl, combine diced mango, red onion, red bell pepper, cilantro, lime juice, salt, and pepper. Mix well.

Set Aside:
- Allow the mango salsa to sit for a few minutes to let the flavors meld.

For the Dipping Sauce (Optional):

Mix Ingredients:
- In a small bowl, mix together sweet chili sauce, soy sauce, and lime juice.

Serve:
- Serve the coconut shrimp with mango salsa on the side, and optionally with the dipping sauce.

Enjoy this delicious and tropical coconut shrimp with mango salsa as an appetizer or main dish!

Air Fried Avocado Fries

Ingredients:

- 2 ripe avocados, sliced into wedges
- 1 cup panko breadcrumbs
- 1/2 cup grated Parmesan cheese
- 1 teaspoon garlic powder
- 1/2 teaspoon smoked paprika
- 1/2 teaspoon salt
- 1/4 teaspoon black pepper
- 2 eggs, beaten
- Cooking spray or oil for misting

Instructions:

Preheat the Air Fryer:
- Preheat your air fryer to 400°F (200°C).

Prepare Breading Station:
- In a shallow dish, combine panko breadcrumbs, grated Parmesan cheese, garlic powder, smoked paprika, salt, and black pepper. Mix well.

Coat Avocado Slices:
- Dip each avocado wedge into the beaten eggs, ensuring it is well-coated.
- Dredge the egg-coated avocado in the breadcrumb mixture, pressing the coating onto the avocado to adhere.

Arrange in the Air Fryer:
- Place the breaded avocado slices in a single layer in the air fryer basket, ensuring they are not touching.

Air Fry:
- Air fry the avocado fries at 400°F (200°C) for 8-10 minutes, flipping halfway through the cooking time. Cook until the coating is golden brown and crispy.

Serve:
- Carefully remove the avocado fries from the air fryer and let them cool for a minute before serving.

Optional Dipping Sauce:
- Serve with your favorite dipping sauce, such as a chipotle mayo, ranch dressing, or a lime-cilantro yogurt sauce.

Enjoy your crispy and delicious air-fried avocado fries as a tasty appetizer or snack!

Eggplant Parmesan Bites

Ingredients:

For the Eggplant Bites:

- 1 medium-sized eggplant, thinly sliced into rounds
- 1 cup all-purpose flour
- 2 large eggs, beaten
- 1 cup Italian-style breadcrumbs
- 1 cup grated Parmesan cheese
- 1 teaspoon dried oregano
- 1 teaspoon dried basil
- 1/2 teaspoon garlic powder
- Salt and black pepper to taste
- Cooking spray or oil for misting

For Assembly:

- Marinara sauce for dipping
- Fresh basil or parsley for garnish (optional)

Instructions:

Preheat the Oven:
- Preheat your oven to 400°F (200°C).

Prepare Breading Station:
- Set up a breading station with three shallow dishes. Place flour in the first dish, beaten eggs in the second, and a mixture of breadcrumbs, grated Parmesan cheese, oregano, basil, garlic powder, salt, and black pepper in the third.

Coat Eggplant Slices:
- Dredge each eggplant round in the flour, dip into the beaten eggs, and coat with the breadcrumb-Parmesan mixture, pressing the coating onto the eggplant to adhere.

Arrange on Baking Sheet:
- Place the breaded eggplant slices on a baking sheet lined with parchment paper or a silicone mat.

Mist with Cooking Spray:
- Lightly mist the tops of the breaded eggplant slices with cooking spray or brush with oil. This helps them crisp up in the oven.

Bake:
- Bake in the preheated oven for 15-20 minutes or until the eggplant bites are golden brown and crispy, flipping them halfway through for even cooking.

Serve:
- Carefully remove the eggplant bites from the oven and let them cool for a minute.

Garnish and Dip:
- Garnish with fresh basil or parsley if desired and serve the eggplant Parmesan bites with marinara sauce for dipping.

These eggplant Parmesan bites make a delightful appetizer or snack, offering all the flavors of classic eggplant Parmesan in a bite-sized form. Enjoy!

Jalapeño Poppers

Ingredients:

- 12 fresh jalapeños
- 8 ounces cream cheese, softened
- 1 cup shredded cheddar or Monterey Jack cheese
- 1 teaspoon garlic powder
- 1/2 teaspoon onion powder
- 1/2 teaspoon smoked paprika
- Salt and black pepper to taste
- 1 cup all-purpose flour
- 2 large eggs, beaten
- 2 cups breadcrumbs (plain or seasoned)
- Cooking spray or oil for misting

Instructions:

Preheat the Oven:
- Preheat your oven to 375°F (190°C).

Prepare the Jalapeños:
- Cut the jalapeños in half lengthwise, and use a spoon to remove the seeds and membranes. Wear gloves to protect your hands from the spice.

Prepare the Filling:
- In a bowl, combine softened cream cheese, shredded cheddar or Monterey Jack cheese, garlic powder, onion powder, smoked paprika, salt, and black pepper. Mix until well combined.

Fill the Jalapeños:
- Spoon the cream cheese mixture into each jalapeño half, filling them evenly.

Breading Station:
- Set up a breading station with three shallow dishes. Place flour in the first dish, beaten eggs in the second, and breadcrumbs in the third.

Coat the Jalapeños:
- Dredge each stuffed jalapeño half in the flour, dip into the beaten eggs, and coat with breadcrumbs, pressing the breadcrumbs onto the jalapeños to adhere.

Arrange on Baking Sheet:
- Place the breaded jalapeño poppers on a baking sheet lined with parchment paper or a silicone mat.

Mist with Cooking Spray:
- Lightly mist the tops of the jalapeño poppers with cooking spray or brush with oil.

Bake:
- Bake in the preheated oven for 20-25 minutes or until the jalapeño poppers are golden brown and the filling is heated through.

Serve:
- Carefully remove the jalapeño poppers from the oven and let them cool for a few minutes before serving.

Jalapeño poppers are best served warm and can be accompanied by dipping sauces like ranch or a cool yogurt-based sauce. Enjoy these spicy and cheesy bites!

Air Fryer Zucchini Chips

Ingredients:

- 2 medium-sized zucchinis, thinly sliced into rounds
- 2 tablespoons olive oil
- 1/2 cup breadcrumbs (panko or regular)
- 1/4 cup grated Parmesan cheese
- 1 teaspoon garlic powder
- 1 teaspoon dried oregano
- 1/2 teaspoon salt
- 1/4 teaspoon black pepper
- Cooking spray or oil for misting

Instructions:

Preheat the Air Fryer:
- Preheat your air fryer to 375°F (190°C).

Prepare the Zucchini:
- Thinly slice the zucchinis into rounds, aiming for about 1/8-inch thickness.

Combine Breadcrumb Mixture:
- In a bowl, combine breadcrumbs, grated Parmesan cheese, garlic powder, dried oregano, salt, and black pepper. Mix well.

Coat Zucchini Slices:
- Toss the zucchini slices with olive oil until they are evenly coated.

Bread the Zucchini:
- Dip each zucchini slice into the breadcrumb mixture, pressing the breadcrumbs onto the zucchini to adhere.

Arrange in the Air Fryer:
- Place the breaded zucchini slices in a single layer in the air fryer basket, ensuring they are not touching. You may need to cook in batches depending on the size of your air fryer.

Mist with Cooking Spray:
- Lightly mist the tops of the zucchini slices with cooking spray or brush with oil.

Air Fry:
- Air fry at 375°F (190°C) for 10-12 minutes, flipping the zucchini slices halfway through, or until they are golden brown and crispy.

Serve:

- Carefully remove the zucchini chips from the air fryer and let them cool for a few minutes before serving.

Enjoy your crispy and flavorful air-fried zucchini chips as a guilt-free snack or a delicious side dish! You can also pair them with a dipping sauce, such as marinara or tzatziki, for added flavor.

Ranch Chicken Tenders

Ingredients:

For the Chicken Tenders:

- 1.5 pounds chicken tenders
- 1 cup buttermilk
- 1 cup all-purpose flour
- 1 teaspoon garlic powder
- 1 teaspoon onion powder
- 1 teaspoon paprika
- 1/2 teaspoon salt
- 1/4 teaspoon black pepper
- Cooking spray or oil for misting

For the Ranch Dipping Sauce:

- 1/2 cup mayonnaise
- 1/2 cup sour cream
- 1 tablespoon fresh chives, chopped
- 1 tablespoon fresh parsley, chopped
- 1 teaspoon dried dill
- 1 teaspoon garlic powder
- 1 teaspoon onion powder
- Salt and black pepper to taste

Instructions:

For the Chicken Tenders:

   Marinate the Chicken:
   - Place the chicken tenders in a bowl and pour the buttermilk over them. Let them marinate for at least 30 minutes or overnight in the refrigerator.

   Prepare the Coating:
   - In a shallow dish, combine the flour, garlic powder, onion powder, paprika, salt, and black pepper. Mix well to ensure even seasoning.

   Coat the Chicken:
   - Preheat your oven to 425°F (220°C).
   - Remove the chicken tenders from the buttermilk, allowing any excess to drip off.
   - Dredge each tender in the flour mixture, ensuring an even coating. Press the flour mixture onto the chicken to help it adhere.

Bake:
- Place the coated chicken tenders on a baking sheet lined with parchment paper. Lightly mist the top of the tenders with cooking spray or brush with oil.
- Bake in the preheated oven for 15-20 minutes or until the chicken is cooked through and golden brown, flipping halfway through the cooking time.

For the Ranch Dipping Sauce:

Prepare the Sauce:
- In a bowl, combine mayonnaise, sour cream, chopped chives, chopped parsley, dried dill, garlic powder, onion powder, salt, and black pepper. Mix well until smooth and well combined.

Serve:
- Serve the ranch chicken tenders hot with the ranch dipping sauce on the side.

Enjoy your flavorful and crispy ranch chicken tenders with a delicious homemade ranch dipping sauce!

Honey Mustard Glazed Salmon

Ingredients:

- 4 salmon fillets
- Salt and black pepper to taste
- 2 tablespoons Dijon mustard
- 2 tablespoons honey
- 1 tablespoon soy sauce
- 1 tablespoon olive oil
- 2 cloves garlic, minced
- 1 tablespoon fresh lemon juice
- Chopped fresh parsley for garnish (optional)
- Lemon wedges for serving

Instructions:

Preheat the Oven:
- Preheat your oven to 400°F (200°C).

Prepare the Salmon:
- Pat the salmon fillets dry with paper towels and season them with salt and black pepper.

Make the Honey Mustard Glaze:
- In a small bowl, whisk together Dijon mustard, honey, soy sauce, olive oil, minced garlic, and fresh lemon juice until well combined.

Coat the Salmon:
- Place the salmon fillets on a baking sheet lined with parchment paper or aluminum foil.
- Brush the honey mustard glaze over each salmon fillet, ensuring they are well coated.

Bake:
- Bake in the preheated oven for 12-15 minutes or until the salmon is cooked through and flakes easily with a fork. The cooking time may vary depending on the thickness of your salmon fillets.

Broil (Optional):
- If you prefer a caramelized top, you can broil the salmon for an additional 2-3 minutes after baking. Keep a close eye to prevent burning.

Garnish and Serve:
- Garnish the honey mustard glazed salmon with chopped fresh parsley if desired.

- Serve the salmon hot with lemon wedges on the side.

This honey mustard glazed salmon is a flavorful and elegant dish that pairs well with a variety of sides, such as roasted vegetables, quinoa, or a fresh green salad. Enjoy your delicious and healthy meal!

Parmesan Crusted Air Fryer Chicken Breast

Ingredients:

- 4 boneless, skinless chicken breasts
- 1 cup grated Parmesan cheese
- 1 cup breadcrumbs (panko or regular)
- 1 teaspoon garlic powder
- 1 teaspoon dried oregano
- 1 teaspoon dried basil
- 1/2 teaspoon smoked paprika
- Salt and black pepper to taste
- 2 eggs, beaten
- Cooking spray or oil for misting

Instructions:

Preheat the Air Fryer:
- Preheat your air fryer to 375°F (190°C).

Prepare Breading Station:
- In a shallow dish, combine grated Parmesan cheese, breadcrumbs, garlic powder, dried oregano, dried basil, smoked paprika, salt, and black pepper. Mix well to create the breading mixture.

Coat the Chicken:
- Pat the chicken breasts dry with paper towels. Dip each chicken breast into the beaten eggs, ensuring they are well-coated.
- Dredge the egg-coated chicken in the Parmesan breadcrumb mixture, pressing the coating onto the chicken to adhere.

Arrange in the Air Fryer:
- Place the breaded chicken breasts in the air fryer basket in a single layer, ensuring they are not touching. You may need to cook in batches.

Mist with Cooking Spray:
- Lightly mist the tops of the chicken breasts with cooking spray or brush with oil. This will help them achieve a golden brown and crispy texture.

Air Fry:
- Air fry at 375°F (190°C) for 18-20 minutes, flipping the chicken breasts halfway through the cooking time, or until they reach an internal temperature of 165°F (74°C).

Serve:

- Carefully remove the Parmesan-crusted chicken breasts from the air fryer and let them rest for a few minutes before serving.

Enjoy your crispy and flavorful Parmesan-crusted air fryer chicken breasts as a tasty main course, paired with your favorite side dishes!

Cinnamon Sugar Air Fryer Donuts

Ingredients:

For the Donuts:

- 1 can (16.3 ounces) refrigerated biscuit dough (flaky, not layered)
- 2 tablespoons unsalted butter, melted

For the Cinnamon Sugar Coating:

- 1/2 cup granulated sugar
- 1 teaspoon ground cinnamon

Instructions:

Preheat the Air Fryer:
- Preheat your air fryer to 350°F (180°C).

Prepare the Biscuit Dough:
- Open the can of refrigerated biscuit dough and separate the biscuits.

Shape the Donuts:
- Use a small round cutter or the back of a piping tip to cut a hole in the center of each biscuit, creating a donut shape. You can also simply use your hands to stretch and shape the biscuits into donut shapes.

Air Fry the Donuts:
- Place the shaped donuts in the preheated air fryer basket in a single layer, ensuring they are not touching. You may need to cook in batches.

Air Fry for 4-6 Minutes:
- Air fry the donuts at 350°F (180°C) for 4-6 minutes or until they are golden brown and cooked through. Cooking times may vary depending on your air fryer, so keep an eye on them.

Melt Butter:
- While the donuts are cooking, melt the unsalted butter in a microwave-safe bowl.

Prepare Cinnamon Sugar Coating:
- In a shallow dish, combine granulated sugar and ground cinnamon to create the cinnamon sugar coating.

Coat the Donuts:
- Once the donuts are cooked, immediately brush each donut with melted butter, then coat them in the cinnamon sugar mixture while they are still warm.

Serve Warm:
- Serve the cinnamon sugar air fryer donuts warm.

Enjoy these quick and delicious cinnamon sugar air fryer donuts as a delightful treat for breakfast or dessert!

Spicy Sweet Potato Wedges

Ingredients:

- 2 large sweet potatoes, washed and cut into wedges
- 2 tablespoons olive oil
- 1 teaspoon paprika
- 1 teaspoon cumin
- 1/2 teaspoon cayenne pepper (adjust to taste for more or less heat)
- 1 teaspoon garlic powder
- 1 teaspoon onion powder
- 1 teaspoon smoked paprika
- Salt and black pepper to taste
- Fresh cilantro or parsley for garnish (optional)

Instructions:

Preheat the Oven:
- Preheat your oven to 400°F (200°C).

Prepare the Sweet Potatoes:
- Wash the sweet potatoes well, and cut them into wedges. Make sure the wedges are of similar size for even cooking.

Season the Wedges:
- In a large bowl, toss the sweet potato wedges with olive oil, paprika, cumin, cayenne pepper, garlic powder, onion powder, smoked paprika, salt, and black pepper. Ensure the wedges are evenly coated with the spices.

Arrange on Baking Sheet:
- Spread the seasoned sweet potato wedges in a single layer on a baking sheet lined with parchment paper.

Bake:
- Bake in the preheated oven for 25-30 minutes, flipping the wedges halfway through, or until the sweet potatoes are tender and golden brown.

Garnish:
- If desired, garnish the spicy sweet potato wedges with fresh cilantro or parsley for a burst of freshness.

Serve:
- Serve the wedges warm as a side dish or snack.

These spicy sweet potato wedges are a delicious and nutritious way to enjoy the goodness of sweet potatoes with a kick of flavor. Enjoy!

Asian-Inspired Sesame Chicken

Ingredients:

For the Chicken:

- 1.5 to 2 pounds boneless, skinless chicken thighs or breasts, cut into bite-sized pieces
- 1/2 cup cornstarch
- Salt and black pepper to taste
- 2 tablespoons vegetable oil, for cooking

For the Sesame Sauce:

- 1/4 cup low-sodium soy sauce
- 2 tablespoons hoisin sauce
- 2 tablespoons rice vinegar
- 2 tablespoons honey or brown sugar
- 1 tablespoon sesame oil
- 2 cloves garlic, minced
- 1 teaspoon ginger, grated
- 1 tablespoon cornstarch (optional, for thickening)
- 2 tablespoons water (optional, for thinning the sauce)

For Garnish:

- Sesame seeds
- Green onions, chopped
- Cooked white or brown rice

Instructions:

Prepare the Chicken:
- In a bowl, season the chicken pieces with salt and black pepper. Coat the chicken pieces with cornstarch, ensuring they are well coated.

Cook the Chicken:
- Heat vegetable oil in a large skillet or wok over medium-high heat. Add the coated chicken pieces and cook until golden brown and cooked through. This may take about 5-7 minutes per side, depending on the size of the chicken pieces. Once cooked, remove the chicken from the skillet and set aside.

Prepare the Sesame Sauce:
- In a small bowl, whisk together soy sauce, hoisin sauce, rice vinegar, honey or brown sugar, sesame oil, minced garlic, and grated ginger. If you prefer a thicker sauce, you can mix 1 tablespoon of cornstarch with 2 tablespoons of water and add it to the sauce.

Combine Chicken and Sauce:
- Return the cooked chicken to the skillet and pour the sesame sauce over it. Toss the chicken until evenly coated and let it simmer for a few minutes until the sauce thickens.

Garnish and Serve:
- Garnish the sesame chicken with sesame seeds and chopped green onions.
- Serve the sesame chicken over cooked rice.

Enjoy your homemade Asian-inspired sesame chicken! The combination of savory and sweet flavors makes this dish a delicious and satisfying meal.

Southwest Egg Rolls

Ingredients:

For the Egg Rolls:

- 1 cup cooked and shredded chicken breast
- 1 cup black beans, drained and rinsed
- 1 cup corn kernels (fresh or frozen)
- 1 cup shredded Monterey Jack cheese
- 1/2 cup diced red bell pepper
- 1/2 cup diced green onions
- 1/4 cup chopped fresh cilantro
- 1 teaspoon ground cumin
- 1 teaspoon chili powder
- 1/2 teaspoon garlic powder
- Salt and black pepper to taste
- 12 egg roll wrappers
- Cooking spray or oil for brushing

For the Dipping Sauce:

- 1/2 cup sour cream
- 2 tablespoons mayonnaise
- 2 tablespoons lime juice
- 1 teaspoon Sriracha sauce (adjust to taste)
- Salt and black pepper to taste

Instructions:

For the Egg Rolls:

Preheat the Oven:
- Preheat your oven to 425°F (220°C).

Prepare Filling:
- In a large bowl, combine shredded chicken, black beans, corn, shredded Monterey Jack cheese, diced red bell pepper, diced green onions, chopped cilantro, ground cumin, chili powder, garlic powder, salt, and black pepper. Mix well.

Assemble the Egg Rolls:

- Place an egg roll wrapper on a clean surface with one corner facing you. Spoon about 2-3 tablespoons of the filling onto the center of the wrapper.
- Fold the bottom corner over the filling, then fold in the sides, and roll tightly.

Seal the Edges:

- Dip your finger in water and moisten the edges of the wrapper to seal the egg roll.

Arrange on Baking Sheet:

- Place the rolled egg rolls on a baking sheet lined with parchment paper, seam side down.

Brush with Oil:

- Lightly brush the tops of the egg rolls with cooking spray or oil.

Bake:

- Bake in the preheated oven for 12-15 minutes or until the egg rolls are golden brown and crispy.

For the Dipping Sauce:

Prepare Sauce:

- In a small bowl, whisk together sour cream, mayonnaise, lime juice, Sriracha sauce, salt, and black pepper. Adjust the Sriracha sauce to your desired level of spiciness.

Serve:

- Serve the Southwest egg rolls hot with the dipping sauce on the side.

Enjoy these delicious Southwest egg rolls as a flavorful appetizer or snack!

Caprese Stuffed Portobello Mushrooms

Ingredients:

- 4 large portobello mushrooms, stems removed
- 2 tablespoons balsamic glaze (store-bought or homemade)
- 2 tablespoons olive oil
- Salt and black pepper to taste

For the Caprese Filling:

- 2 large tomatoes, sliced
- 8 ounces fresh mozzarella, sliced
- Fresh basil leaves
- Balsamic glaze for drizzling (optional)

Instructions:

Preheat the Oven:
- Preheat your oven to 400°F (200°C).

Prepare Portobello Mushrooms:
- Clean the portobello mushrooms and remove the stems. Use a spoon to gently scrape out the gills from the inside of the mushrooms, creating a well for the filling.

Brush with Olive Oil:
- Brush the outside of each mushroom with olive oil and season with salt and black pepper.

Roast the Mushrooms:
- Place the mushrooms on a baking sheet, gill side up, and roast in the preheated oven for about 10 minutes to soften them slightly.

Prepare Caprese Filling:
- While the mushrooms are roasting, prepare the caprese filling. Layer slices of tomato, fresh mozzarella, and basil leaves inside each mushroom cap.

Drizzle with Balsamic Glaze:
- Drizzle balsamic glaze over the caprese filling. If you don't have balsamic glaze, you can use a reduction of balsamic vinegar.

Continue Roasting:
- Return the stuffed mushrooms to the oven and continue roasting for an additional 10-15 minutes or until the mushrooms are tender, and the cheese is melted and bubbly.

Serve:
- Carefully remove the stuffed portobello mushrooms from the oven and transfer them to a serving platter.
- Drizzle with additional balsamic glaze if desired.

Garnish:
- Garnish with fresh basil leaves before serving.

These caprese stuffed portobello mushrooms make a delightful appetizer or a light main course. Enjoy the rich flavors of this classic combination!

Bacon-Wrapped Jalapeño Poppers

Ingredients:

- 12 large jalapeño peppers
- 8 ounces cream cheese, softened
- 1 cup shredded cheddar or Monterey Jack cheese
- 1 teaspoon garlic powder
- 1/2 teaspoon onion powder
- 1/2 teaspoon smoked paprika
- Salt and black pepper to taste
- 12 slices of bacon, cut in half
- Toothpicks

Instructions:

Preheat the Oven:
- Preheat your oven to 375°F (190°C).

Prepare the Jalapeños:
- Cut the jalapeños in half lengthwise and remove the seeds and membranes. Wear gloves to protect your hands from the spice.

Prepare the Filling:
- In a bowl, mix together softened cream cheese, shredded cheddar or Monterey Jack cheese, garlic powder, onion powder, smoked paprika, salt, and black pepper. Mix until well combined.

Fill the Jalapeños:
- Spoon the cream cheese mixture into each jalapeño half, filling them evenly.

Wrap with Bacon:
- Wrap each cream cheese-filled jalapeño with a half-slice of bacon, ensuring it covers the entire length of the pepper.

Secure with Toothpicks:
- Secure the bacon-wrapped jalapeños with toothpicks, making sure to insert them through the ends of the bacon to prevent unwrapping during cooking.

Bake:
- Place the bacon-wrapped jalapeño poppers on a baking sheet lined with parchment paper or a baking rack.
- Bake in the preheated oven for 20-25 minutes or until the bacon is crispy and the jalapeños are tender.

Broil (Optional):
- If you prefer crispier bacon, you can broil the poppers for an additional 2-3 minutes, but keep a close eye to prevent burning.

Serve:
- Carefully remove the bacon-wrapped jalapeño poppers from the oven and let them cool for a few minutes before serving.

These bacon-wrapped jalapeño poppers make a fantastic appetizer for parties or game day gatherings. Enjoy the combination of creamy, spicy, and smoky flavors!

Air Fryer Teriyaki Tofu

Ingredients:

For the Teriyaki Marinade:

- 1/4 cup soy sauce
- 2 tablespoons mirin (sweet rice wine)
- 2 tablespoons rice vinegar
- 2 tablespoons brown sugar
- 1 tablespoon grated ginger
- 2 cloves garlic, minced
- 1 tablespoon cornstarch (optional, for thickening)

For the Tofu:

- 1 block extra-firm tofu, pressed and cubed
- 2 tablespoons cornstarch
- 1 tablespoon vegetable oil

Optional Garnish:

- Sesame seeds
- Chopped green onions

Instructions:

For the Teriyaki Marinade:

    Prepare the Marinade:
- In a small saucepan, combine soy sauce, mirin, rice vinegar, brown sugar, grated ginger, and minced garlic. Whisk together over medium heat until the sugar dissolves.
- If you prefer a thicker sauce, mix cornstarch with a little water to create a slurry and add it to the sauce. Cook, stirring, until the sauce thickens. Remove from heat.

    Marinate the Tofu:
- Cut the pressed tofu into cubes and place them in a shallow dish.
- Pour a portion of the teriyaki marinade over the tofu, reserving some for later. Allow the tofu to marinate for at least 15-30 minutes.

For the Air-Fried Tofu:

Coat Tofu with Cornstarch:
- Preheat your air fryer to 375°F (190°C).
- Toss the marinated tofu cubes with cornstarch until they are evenly coated.

Air Fry:
- Lightly grease the air fryer basket with vegetable oil.
- Arrange the tofu cubes in a single layer in the air fryer basket, ensuring they are not touching. You may need to cook in batches.
- Air fry for 15-20 minutes, shaking the basket or flipping the tofu halfway through, until the tofu is golden brown and crispy.

Glaze with Teriyaki Sauce:
- In the last 5 minutes of cooking, brush or drizzle the reserved teriyaki sauce over the tofu cubes for a flavorful glaze.

Serve:
- Carefully remove the air-fried teriyaki tofu from the air fryer and serve hot.
- Garnish with sesame seeds and chopped green onions if desired.

Enjoy your air-fried teriyaki tofu as a tasty and plant-based main course or as a flavorful addition to salads and rice bowls!

Garlic Herb Air Fryer Pork Chops

Ingredients:

For the Pork Chops:

- 4 bone-in pork chops, about 1 inch thick
- Salt and black pepper to taste

For the Garlic Herb Marinade:

- 3 tablespoons olive oil
- 4 cloves garlic, minced
- 1 teaspoon dried thyme
- 1 teaspoon dried rosemary
- 1 teaspoon dried oregano
- 1 teaspoon paprika
- 1/2 teaspoon onion powder
- 1/2 teaspoon dried sage (optional)
- 1/2 teaspoon dried marjoram (optional)

Instructions:

Preheat the Air Fryer:
- Preheat your air fryer to 375°F (190°C).

Prepare the Marinade:
- In a small bowl, whisk together olive oil, minced garlic, dried thyme, dried rosemary, dried oregano, paprika, onion powder, dried sage (if using), and dried marjoram (if using).

Marinate the Pork Chops:
- Pat the pork chops dry with paper towels and season them with salt and black pepper.
- Brush both sides of the pork chops with the garlic herb marinade, ensuring they are well coated.

Arrange in the Air Fryer:
- Place the marinated pork chops in the air fryer basket in a single layer, ensuring they are not touching. You may need to cook in batches depending on the size of your air fryer.

Air Fry:

- Air fry at 375°F (190°C) for 12-15 minutes, flipping the pork chops halfway through, or until they reach an internal temperature of 145°F (63°C) for medium doneness.

Rest and Serve:
- Allow the pork chops to rest for a few minutes before serving to allow the juices to redistribute.
- Serve the garlic herb air fryer pork chops hot.

These garlic herb air fryer pork chops are deliciously seasoned and cook up quickly in the air fryer, making them a perfect weeknight dinner option. Enjoy the flavorful combination of herbs and garlic!

Mediterranean Stuffed Peppers

Ingredients:

For the Stuffed Peppers:

- 4 large bell peppers, halved and seeds removed
- 1 cup cooked quinoa or couscous
- 1 cup cherry tomatoes, halved
- 1 cup cucumber, diced
- 1/2 cup Kalamata olives, sliced
- 1/2 cup crumbled feta cheese
- 1/4 cup red onion, finely chopped
- 2 tablespoons fresh parsley, chopped
- 2 tablespoons fresh mint, chopped
- 1 tablespoon olive oil
- Salt and black pepper to taste

For the Lemon Vinaigrette:

- 3 tablespoons olive oil
- 2 tablespoons fresh lemon juice
- 1 teaspoon Dijon mustard
- 1 clove garlic, minced
- Salt and black pepper to taste

Instructions:

For the Stuffed Peppers:

    Preheat the Oven:
- Preheat your oven to 375°F (190°C).

    Prepare the Peppers:
- Cut the bell peppers in half lengthwise and remove the seeds and membranes.

    Prepare the Filling:
- In a large bowl, combine cooked quinoa or couscous, cherry tomatoes, cucumber, Kalamata olives, feta cheese, red onion, fresh parsley, fresh mint, and olive oil. Toss to combine.
- Season the filling with salt and black pepper to taste.

    Stuff the Peppers:
- Spoon the quinoa mixture into each bell pepper half, pressing it down slightly.

    Bake:

- Place the stuffed peppers in a baking dish or on a baking sheet.
- Bake in the preheated oven for 25-30 minutes or until the peppers are tender.

For the Lemon Vinaigrette:

Prepare the Vinaigrette:
- In a small bowl, whisk together olive oil, fresh lemon juice, Dijon mustard, minced garlic, salt, and black pepper.

Drizzle and Serve:
- Drizzle the lemon vinaigrette over the stuffed peppers before serving.

Garnish:
- Garnish the Mediterranean stuffed peppers with additional fresh herbs if desired.

Serve these Mediterranean stuffed peppers as a light and colorful main course or a delicious side dish. Enjoy the vibrant flavors of the Mediterranean!

Crispy Coconut Chicken Strips

Ingredients:

For the Coconut Chicken Strips:

- 1.5 pounds boneless, skinless chicken breast, cut into strips
- 1 cup shredded coconut (unsweetened)
- 1 cup panko breadcrumbs
- 1/2 cup all-purpose flour
- 2 large eggs, beaten
- 1 teaspoon garlic powder
- 1 teaspoon onion powder
- Salt and black pepper to taste
- Cooking spray or vegetable oil for misting

For the Dipping Sauce:

- 1/2 cup plain Greek yogurt
- 2 tablespoons honey
- 1 tablespoon Dijon mustard
- 1 tablespoon lime juice
- Salt and black pepper to taste

Instructions:

For the Coconut Chicken Strips:

Preheat the Oven:
- Preheat your oven to 400°F (200°C).

Prepare the Breading Station:
- In one bowl, place shredded coconut. In another bowl, mix panko breadcrumbs with garlic powder, onion powder, salt, and black pepper. In a third bowl, add all-purpose flour.

Coat the Chicken Strips:
- Dredge each chicken strip in the flour, shaking off any excess. Then dip it into the beaten eggs, allowing any excess to drip off. Finally, coat the chicken strip in the shredded coconut and breadcrumb mixture, pressing it on to adhere.

Arrange on Baking Sheet:
- Place the coated chicken strips on a baking sheet lined with parchment paper, ensuring they are not touching.

Mist with Cooking Spray:

- Lightly mist the tops of the coconut-coated chicken strips with cooking spray or brush with vegetable oil. This will help them become crispy during baking.

Bake:
- Bake in the preheated oven for 20-25 minutes or until the chicken is cooked through and the coating is golden brown and crispy.

For the Dipping Sauce:

Prepare the Sauce:
- In a small bowl, whisk together Greek yogurt, honey, Dijon mustard, lime juice, salt, and black pepper until well combined.

Serve:
- Serve the crispy coconut chicken strips hot with the dipping sauce on the side.

Enjoy these crispy coconut chicken strips as a delightful main course or a crowd-pleasing appetizer!

Air Fryer Shrimp Tacos

Ingredients:

For the Air-Fried Shrimp:

- 1 pound large shrimp, peeled and deveined
- 1 cup panko breadcrumbs
- 1 teaspoon smoked paprika
- 1 teaspoon garlic powder
- 1/2 teaspoon onion powder
- 1/2 teaspoon cayenne pepper (adjust to taste)
- Salt and black pepper to taste
- 2 large eggs, beaten
- Cooking spray or oil for misting

For the Taco Assembly:

- 8 small flour or corn tortillas
- Shredded lettuce
- Diced tomatoes
- Sliced red onions
- Sliced jalapeños
- Chopped cilantro
- Lime wedges

Optional Toppings:

- Shredded cheese
- Guacamole
- Sour cream

Instructions:

For the Air-Fried Shrimp:

Preheat the Air Fryer:
- Preheat your air fryer to 375°F (190°C).

Prepare the Shrimp Coating:
- In a bowl, mix together panko breadcrumbs, smoked paprika, garlic powder, onion powder, cayenne pepper, salt, and black pepper.

Coat the Shrimp:

- Dip each shrimp into the beaten eggs and then coat it with the breadcrumb mixture, pressing the breadcrumbs onto the shrimp to adhere.

Arrange in the Air Fryer:
- Place the coated shrimp in the air fryer basket in a single layer. Lightly mist the tops with cooking spray or brush with oil.

Air Fry:
- Air fry for 8-10 minutes, flipping the shrimp halfway through, or until the shrimp are golden brown and cooked through.

For Taco Assembly:

Warm the Tortillas:
- While the shrimp are cooking, warm the tortillas according to package instructions or preference.

Assemble the Tacos:
- Place a layer of shredded lettuce on each tortilla.
- Top with air-fried shrimp and add your favorite taco toppings, such as diced tomatoes, sliced red onions, sliced jalapeños, chopped cilantro, and a squeeze of lime juice.

Optional Toppings:
- If desired, add additional toppings like shredded cheese, guacamole, or sour cream.

Serve:
- Serve the air fryer shrimp tacos hot with your favorite toppings.

Enjoy these delicious air fryer shrimp tacos as a quick and satisfying meal!

Lemon Garlic Butter Shrimp

Ingredients:

- 1 pound large shrimp, peeled and deveined
- Salt and black pepper to taste
- 2 tablespoons olive oil
- 4 cloves garlic, minced
- 1/2 teaspoon red pepper flakes (optional, for heat)
- 1/2 cup chicken or vegetable broth
- Juice of 1 lemon
- Zest of 1 lemon
- 2 tablespoons unsalted butter
- 2 tablespoons fresh parsley, chopped

Instructions:

Prepare the Shrimp:
- Pat the shrimp dry with paper towels and season with salt and black pepper.

Sauté Shrimp:
- In a large skillet, heat olive oil over medium-high heat. Add the shrimp to the skillet and cook for 1-2 minutes per side or until they start to turn pink. Remove the shrimp from the skillet and set aside.

Sauté Garlic and Red Pepper Flakes:
- In the same skillet, add minced garlic and red pepper flakes (if using). Sauté for about 1 minute until the garlic becomes fragrant.

Deglaze with Broth:
- Pour in the chicken or vegetable broth, scraping any browned bits from the bottom of the skillet with a spatula.

Add Lemon Juice and Zest:
- Add the lemon juice and lemon zest to the skillet. Stir well to combine.

Finish with Butter:
- Reduce the heat to medium and add the unsalted butter to the skillet. Stir until the butter is melted and the sauce is well combined.

Return Shrimp to the Skillet:
- Return the cooked shrimp to the skillet, tossing them in the lemon garlic butter sauce. Cook for an additional 1-2 minutes until the shrimp are fully coated and heated through.

Garnish and Serve:

- Garnish the lemon garlic butter shrimp with fresh chopped parsley.
- Serve the shrimp over cooked pasta, rice, or with crusty bread to soak up the delicious sauce.

Enjoy your lemon garlic butter shrimp with its vibrant and zesty flavors!

Sweet and Spicy Chicken Drumsticks

Ingredients:

For the Chicken Marinade:

- 2 pounds chicken drumsticks
- 1/4 cup soy sauce
- 1/4 cup honey
- 2 tablespoons olive oil
- 2 cloves garlic, minced
- 1 teaspoon grated ginger
- 1 teaspoon smoked paprika
- 1/2 teaspoon cayenne pepper (adjust to taste for spice)
- Salt and black pepper to taste

For Garnish (Optional):

- Sesame seeds
- Chopped green onions
- Sliced red chili peppers

Instructions:

Prepare the Chicken:
- In a bowl, whisk together soy sauce, honey, olive oil, minced garlic, grated ginger, smoked paprika, cayenne pepper, salt, and black pepper to create the marinade.

Marinate the Chicken:
- Place the chicken drumsticks in a large zip-top bag or a shallow dish. Pour the marinade over the chicken, ensuring it's evenly coated. Marinate in the refrigerator for at least 30 minutes to allow the flavors to meld.

Preheat the Oven:
- Preheat your oven to 400°F (200°C).

Arrange on a Baking Sheet:
- Line a baking sheet with parchment paper or aluminum foil. Place a wire rack on top of the baking sheet.

Place Drumsticks on Rack:
- Remove the chicken drumsticks from the marinade, allowing any excess to drip off. Place the drumsticks on the wire rack.

Bake:

- Bake in the preheated oven for 35-40 minutes or until the chicken is cooked through, and the skin is crispy. You can also broil for the last few minutes to enhance crispiness.

Garnish (Optional):
- Garnish the sweet and spicy chicken drumsticks with sesame seeds, chopped green onions, and sliced red chili peppers if desired.

Serve:
- Serve the chicken drumsticks hot as a delicious and flavorful main course.

Enjoy these sweet and spicy chicken drumsticks with a perfect balance of flavors! They make a great dish for family dinners or gatherings.

Pesto Zoodle (Zucchini Noodle) Bowl

Ingredients:

For the Pesto:

- 2 cups fresh basil leaves, packed
- 1/2 cup grated Parmesan cheese
- 1/2 cup pine nuts or walnuts
- 3 garlic cloves, peeled
- 1/2 cup extra-virgin olive oil
- Salt and black pepper to taste
- 1 tablespoon lemon juice (optional)

For the Zoodle Bowl:

- 4 medium-sized zucchinis, spiralized into noodles
- Cherry tomatoes, halved
- Fresh mozzarella balls (bocconcini), halved
- Kalamata olives, sliced
- Pine nuts, toasted (optional)
- Salt and black pepper to taste
- Extra Parmesan cheese for garnish (optional)

Instructions:

For the Pesto:

Prepare the Pesto:
- In a food processor, combine fresh basil, grated Parmesan cheese, pine nuts or walnuts, and peeled garlic cloves.
- Pulse until the ingredients are finely chopped.

Add Olive Oil:
- With the food processor running, slowly pour in the extra-virgin olive oil until the pesto reaches your desired consistency.

Season and Adjust:
- Season the pesto with salt and black pepper to taste. If desired, add lemon juice for a hint of brightness.
- Taste and adjust the seasoning as needed.

For the Zoodle Bowl:

Prepare Zucchini Noodles:
- Spiralize the zucchinis into noodles using a spiralizer. If you don't have a spiralizer, you can use a vegetable peeler to create thin ribbons.

Sauté Zoodles:
- Heat a large skillet over medium heat. Add a little olive oil, then sauté the zucchini noodles for 2-3 minutes until they are just tender. Be careful not to overcook them.

Assemble the Bowl:
- In a bowl, toss the sautéed zucchini noodles with cherry tomatoes, fresh mozzarella balls, sliced Kalamata olives, and toasted pine nuts if desired.

Add Pesto:
- Spoon the homemade pesto over the zoodle mixture. Toss until the noodles are well coated with the pesto.

Season:
- Season the pesto zoodle bowl with salt and black pepper to taste.

Garnish and Serve:
- Garnish with extra Parmesan cheese if desired.
- Serve the pesto zoodle bowl warm or at room temperature.

This pesto zoodle bowl is a refreshing and nutritious option for a light lunch or dinner. Enjoy the vibrant flavors and textures of this low-carb dish!

Air Fried Pickles

Ingredients:

- 1 jar of dill pickle slices or spears, drained
- 1 cup all-purpose flour
- 2 teaspoons paprika
- 1 teaspoon garlic powder
- 1 teaspoon onion powder
- 1/2 teaspoon cayenne pepper (adjust to taste)
- Salt and black pepper to taste
- 2 large eggs
- 1 cup panko breadcrumbs
- Cooking spray

Instructions:

Preheat the Air Fryer:
- Preheat your air fryer to 400°F (200°C).

Prepare Breading Station:
- In one bowl, combine flour, paprika, garlic powder, onion powder, cayenne pepper, salt, and black pepper. In another bowl, beat the eggs. Place panko breadcrumbs in a third bowl.

Coat Pickles:
- Dip each pickle slice or spear into the flour mixture, ensuring it is well-coated. Shake off any excess flour.
- Dip the coated pickle into the beaten eggs, allowing any excess to drip off.
- Finally, coat the pickle with panko breadcrumbs, pressing the breadcrumbs onto the pickle to adhere.

Arrange in Air Fryer Basket:
- Place the breaded pickles in a single layer in the air fryer basket, ensuring they are not touching.

Air Fry:
- Lightly spray the coated pickles with cooking spray.
- Air fry for 8-10 minutes, flipping the pickles halfway through, or until they are golden brown and crispy.

Serve:
- Carefully remove the air-fried pickles from the air fryer and serve them hot.

Dipping Sauce (Optional):

- Mix mayonnaise and a splash of hot sauce for a spicy dipping sauce.
- Combine ranch dressing with a squeeze of lemon juice for a tangy option.

Enjoy these air-fried pickles as a tasty snack or appetizer. The crispy exterior and tangy pickle flavor make them a delightful treat!

Apple Cinnamon Air Fryer Pancakes

Ingredients:

- 1 cup all-purpose flour
- 1 tablespoon sugar
- 1 teaspoon baking powder
- 1/2 teaspoon baking soda
- 1/4 teaspoon salt
- 1 teaspoon ground cinnamon
- 3/4 cup buttermilk
- 1 large egg
- 1 tablespoon melted butter
- 1 teaspoon vanilla extract
- 1 medium apple, peeled, cored, and finely chopped

Instructions:

Preheat the Air Fryer:
- Preheat your air fryer to 350°F (180°C).

Prepare the Batter:
- In a mixing bowl, whisk together the flour, sugar, baking powder, baking soda, salt, and ground cinnamon.

Mix Wet Ingredients:
- In another bowl, whisk together the buttermilk, egg, melted butter, and vanilla extract.

Combine Wet and Dry Ingredients:
- Pour the wet ingredients into the dry ingredients and stir until just combined. Do not overmix; it's okay if there are a few lumps.

Add Chopped Apples:
- Gently fold in the finely chopped apple into the pancake batter.

Grease the Air Fryer Basket:
- Lightly grease the air fryer basket or use parchment paper to prevent sticking.

Spoon Pancake Batter:
- Drop spoonfuls of pancake batter onto the air fryer basket, leaving space between each pancake.

Air Fry:
- Air fry the pancakes at 350°F (180°C) for about 4-5 minutes. Check the pancakes halfway through and flip them if needed.

Serve:
- Once the pancakes are golden brown and cooked through, remove them from the air fryer.

Optional Toppings:
- Serve the apple cinnamon pancakes warm with your favorite toppings, such as maple syrup, whipped cream, or additional apple slices.

Enjoy these quick and tasty air fryer apple cinnamon pancakes for a delightful breakfast treat!

Blackened Salmon Tacos

Ingredients:

For the Blackened Salmon:

- 1 pound salmon fillets, skinless
- 1 tablespoon olive oil
- 1 tablespoon blackening seasoning
- 1 teaspoon smoked paprika
- 1 teaspoon garlic powder
- 1 teaspoon onion powder
- 1/2 teaspoon dried thyme
- 1/2 teaspoon dried oregano
- 1/2 teaspoon cayenne pepper (adjust to taste)
- Salt and black pepper to taste
- Lime wedges for serving

For the Tacos:

- 8 small flour or corn tortillas
- Shredded lettuce
- Diced tomatoes
- Sliced red onions
- Avocado slices
- Fresh cilantro, chopped
- Sour cream or Greek yogurt for topping

Instructions:

For the Blackened Salmon:

    Prepare the Blackening Seasoning:
- In a small bowl, mix together blackening seasoning, smoked paprika, garlic powder, onion powder, dried thyme, dried oregano, cayenne pepper, salt, and black pepper.

    Coat the Salmon:
- Brush the salmon fillets with olive oil and generously coat them with the blackening seasoning mixture.

    Preheat the Pan:
- Heat a skillet or grill pan over medium-high heat.

Cook the Salmon:
- Place the seasoned salmon fillets in the hot pan and cook for 3-4 minutes per side or until the salmon is cooked through and has a blackened crust.

Flake the Salmon:
- Once cooked, flake the salmon into bite-sized pieces using a fork.

For Assembling Tacos:

Warm the Tortillas:
- Heat the tortillas according to package instructions or preference.

Assemble Tacos:
- Fill each warm tortilla with shredded lettuce, diced tomatoes, sliced red onions, avocado slices, and the flaked blackened salmon.

Add Toppings:
- Top the tacos with fresh cilantro and a dollop of sour cream or Greek yogurt.

Serve:
- Serve the blackened salmon tacos with lime wedges on the side.

Enjoy these flavorful blackened salmon tacos for a delicious and satisfying meal!

Cheesy Broccoli Bites

Ingredients:

- 2 cups broccoli florets, steamed and finely chopped
- 1 cup shredded cheddar cheese
- 1/2 cup breadcrumbs
- 1/4 cup grated Parmesan cheese
- 2 large eggs
- 2 cloves garlic, minced
- 1 teaspoon dried oregano
- 1/2 teaspoon onion powder
- Salt and black pepper to taste
- Cooking spray

Instructions:

Preheat the Oven:
- Preheat your oven to 375°F (190°C).

Prepare the Broccoli:
- Steam the broccoli florets until tender, then finely chop them.

Combine Ingredients:
- In a large bowl, combine the chopped broccoli, shredded cheddar cheese, breadcrumbs, grated Parmesan cheese, eggs, minced garlic, dried oregano, onion powder, salt, and black pepper. Mix until well combined.

Shape into Bites:
- Scoop a tablespoon-sized portion of the mixture and shape it into a bite-sized ball. Place it on a baking sheet lined with parchment paper.

Bake:
- Repeat the process until all the mixture is used.
- Lightly spray the tops of the broccoli bites with cooking spray to help them brown.
- Bake in the preheated oven for 15-20 minutes or until the edges are golden brown.

Serve:
- Allow the cheesy broccoli bites to cool for a few minutes before serving.

Optional Dipping Sauce:
- Serve with your favorite dipping sauce, such as marinara, ranch, or a yogurt-based dip.

Enjoy these cheesy broccoli bites as a tasty and satisfying snack or appetizer. They're a great way to sneak some vegetables into your diet!

Maple Glazed Bacon-Wrapped Dates

Ingredients:

- 16 large Medjool dates, pitted
- 8 slices of bacon, cut in half
- 1/4 cup maple syrup
- 1/4 teaspoon cayenne pepper (optional, for a hint of heat)
- Toothpicks

Instructions:

Preheat the Oven:
- Preheat your oven to 375°F (190°C).

Prepare the Dates:
- Make a small slit in each date and remove the pit.

Prepare the Glaze:
- In a small bowl, mix together the maple syrup and cayenne pepper (if using). This creates a sweet and slightly spicy glaze.

Wrap Dates with Bacon:
- Take a half-slice of bacon and wrap it around each date. Secure the bacon with a toothpick, ensuring it goes through the bacon and the date to hold them together.

Arrange on Baking Sheet:
- Place the bacon-wrapped dates on a baking sheet lined with parchment paper, leaving some space between each one.

Brush with Glaze:
- Using a brush or spoon, generously brush each bacon-wrapped date with the maple syrup glaze.

Bake:
- Bake in the preheated oven for 15-20 minutes or until the bacon is crispy and caramelized.

Serve:
- Remove the toothpicks before serving.

Optional:
- Serve these delightful appetizers as is, or try stuffing them with goat cheese or almonds for an extra layer of flavor.

Maple-glazed bacon-wrapped dates are perfect for serving at parties or as a delicious appetizer before a meal. Enjoy the sweet and savory goodness!

Coconut Crusted Tilapia

Ingredients:

For the Coconut Crust:

- 4 tilapia fillets
- 1 cup shredded coconut (unsweetened)
- 1/2 cup panko breadcrumbs
- 1/2 teaspoon garlic powder
- 1/2 teaspoon onion powder
- 1/2 teaspoon paprika
- Salt and black pepper to taste
- 2 large eggs, beaten

For Serving:

- Lime wedges
- Fresh cilantro, chopped
- Optional: Sweet chili sauce or mango salsa for dipping

Instructions:

Preheat the Oven:
- Preheat your oven to 400°F (200°C).

Prepare the Tilapia:
- Pat the tilapia fillets dry with paper towels.

Coconut Crust Mixture:
- In a shallow bowl, combine shredded coconut, panko breadcrumbs, garlic powder, onion powder, paprika, salt, and black pepper. Mix well.

Dip in Beaten Eggs:
- Dip each tilapia fillet into the beaten eggs, ensuring both sides are coated.

Coat with Coconut Mixture:
- Press the egg-coated tilapia fillet into the coconut crust mixture, ensuring it is well coated on both sides.

Place on Baking Sheet:
- Place the coated tilapia fillets on a baking sheet lined with parchment paper.

Bake:
- Bake in the preheated oven for 12-15 minutes or until the tilapia is cooked through and the coconut crust is golden brown and crispy.

Serve:
- Serve the coconut-crusted tilapia hot with lime wedges and a sprinkle of fresh chopped cilantro.

Optional Dipping Sauce:
- Serve with sweet chili sauce or mango salsa for a sweet and tangy accompaniment.

Enjoy this coconut-crusted tilapia for a tropical and satisfying meal that's quick and easy to prepare!

Air Fryer Corn on the Cob

Ingredients:

- 4 ears of corn, husks and silks removed
- Olive oil or melted butter
- Salt and black pepper to taste

Instructions:

Preheat the Air Fryer:
- Preheat your air fryer to 400°F (200°C).

Prepare the Corn:
- Peel back the husks of the corn without removing them. Remove the silks and then fold the husks back over the corn.

Brush with Oil or Butter:
- Lightly brush each ear of corn with olive oil or melted butter. This will enhance the flavor and help the seasoning stick.

Season:
- Sprinkle salt and black pepper over the corn to taste. You can also experiment with other seasonings like garlic powder, paprika, or chili powder if desired.

Arrange in the Air Fryer:
- Place the prepared corn on the cob directly in the air fryer basket. Depending on the size of your air fryer, you may need to cook the corn in batches.

Air Fry:
- Air fry the corn at 400°F (200°C) for 12-15 minutes, turning halfway through the cooking time. The corn should be golden brown and cooked to your desired tenderness.

Serve:
- Once done, remove the corn from the air fryer. Let it cool for a minute, then peel back the husks and enjoy.

Optional Grilling Finish (Optional):
- For a smoky flavor, you can transfer the air-fried corn to a preheated grill for a few minutes to get grill marks and extra char.

Serve the air-fried corn on the cob with additional butter, seasoning, or your favorite toppings. It's a simple and delicious side dish that's perfect for summer meals or barbecues.

Chicken Parmesan Meatballs

Ingredients:

For the Meatballs:

- 1 pound ground chicken
- 1/2 cup breadcrumbs
- 1/4 cup grated Parmesan cheese
- 1/4 cup chopped fresh parsley
- 1/4 cup finely chopped onion
- 2 cloves garlic, minced
- 1 large egg
- 1 teaspoon dried oregano
- 1 teaspoon dried basil
- Salt and black pepper to taste
- Olive oil for cooking

For the Sauce:

- 2 cups marinara sauce
- 1/2 teaspoon dried oregano
- 1/2 teaspoon dried basil

For Assembly:

- 1 cup shredded mozzarella cheese
- 1/4 cup grated Parmesan cheese
- Fresh basil or parsley for garnish

Instructions:

For the Meatballs:

Preheat the Oven:
- Preheat your oven to 375°F (190°C).

Prepare the Meatball Mixture:
- In a large bowl, combine ground chicken, breadcrumbs, grated Parmesan, chopped parsley, chopped onion, minced garlic, egg, dried oregano, dried basil, salt, and black pepper. Mix until well combined.

Shape the Meatballs:

- Shape the mixture into meatballs, about 1-2 inches in diameter.

Cook the Meatballs:
- Heat olive oil in a large oven-safe skillet over medium-high heat. Brown the meatballs on all sides, but they don't need to be fully cooked as they will finish cooking in the oven.

Prepare the Sauce:
- In a small bowl, mix together the marinara sauce, dried oregano, and dried basil.

Add Sauce and Bake:
- Pour the marinara sauce over the browned meatballs in the skillet. Sprinkle with shredded mozzarella and grated Parmesan cheese.

Bake in the Oven:
- Transfer the skillet to the preheated oven and bake for 15-20 minutes or until the meatballs are cooked through, and the cheese is melted and bubbly.

Garnish and Serve:
- Garnish with fresh basil or parsley before serving.

Serve these chicken Parmesan meatballs over pasta or with crusty bread for a delicious and satisfying meal. Enjoy the rich flavors of chicken Parmesan in a bite-sized form!

Cajun Sweet Potato Fries

Ingredients:

- 2 large sweet potatoes, peeled and cut into fries
- 2 tablespoons olive oil
- 1 tablespoon Cajun seasoning
- 1 teaspoon smoked paprika
- 1/2 teaspoon garlic powder
- 1/2 teaspoon onion powder
- 1/2 teaspoon dried thyme
- 1/2 teaspoon cayenne pepper (adjust to taste)
- Salt and black pepper to taste
- Fresh parsley or cilantro for garnish (optional)

Instructions:

Preheat the Oven:
- Preheat your oven to 425°F (220°C).

Prepare the Sweet Potatoes:
- Peel the sweet potatoes and cut them into evenly sized fries.

Seasoning Mixture:
- In a large bowl, mix together olive oil, Cajun seasoning, smoked paprika, garlic powder, onion powder, dried thyme, cayenne pepper, salt, and black pepper.

Coat the Fries:
- Toss the sweet potato fries in the seasoning mixture until they are evenly coated.

Arrange on Baking Sheet:
- Arrange the seasoned sweet potato fries in a single layer on a baking sheet lined with parchment paper, ensuring they are not overcrowded.

Bake:
- Bake in the preheated oven for 20-25 minutes, flipping the fries halfway through, or until the fries are golden brown and crispy.

Garnish and Serve:
- Garnish the Cajun sweet potato fries with fresh parsley or cilantro if desired.

Optional Dipping Sauce:
- Serve with a dipping sauce of your choice, such as spicy mayo, aioli, or ranch.

Enjoy these Cajun sweet potato fries as a flavorful and slightly spicy side dish or snack. They're a perfect alternative to regular fries and add a unique twist to your meals!

Mediterranean Chickpea Salad

Ingredients:

For the Salad:

- 2 cans (15 oz each) chickpeas, drained and rinsed
- 1 cucumber, diced
- 1 cup cherry tomatoes, halved
- 1/2 red onion, finely chopped
- 1/2 cup Kalamata olives, pitted and sliced
- 1/2 cup feta cheese, crumbled
- 1/4 cup fresh parsley, chopped

For the Dressing:

- 1/4 cup extra-virgin olive oil
- 2 tablespoons red wine vinegar
- 1 teaspoon Dijon mustard
- 1 clove garlic, minced
- 1 teaspoon dried oregano
- Salt and black pepper to taste

Instructions:

Prepare the Chickpeas:
- Drain and rinse the chickpeas under cold water. Pat them dry with a paper towel.

Assemble the Salad:
- In a large salad bowl, combine the chickpeas, diced cucumber, halved cherry tomatoes, finely chopped red onion, sliced Kalamata olives, crumbled feta cheese, and chopped fresh parsley.

Prepare the Dressing:
- In a small bowl, whisk together the extra-virgin olive oil, red wine vinegar, Dijon mustard, minced garlic, dried oregano, salt, and black pepper.

Toss the Salad:
- Pour the dressing over the salad ingredients and toss everything together until well coated.

Chill (Optional):
- If time allows, refrigerate the salad for 30 minutes to allow the flavors to meld.

Serve:
- Serve the Mediterranean chickpea salad chilled or at room temperature.

This Mediterranean chickpea salad is a versatile dish that can be served as a light lunch, a side dish, or a healthy snack. Enjoy the combination of chickpeas, fresh vegetables, and flavorful dressing for a taste of the Mediterranean!

Teriyaki Pineapple Chicken Skewers

Ingredients:

For the Teriyaki Marinade:

- 1/2 cup soy sauce
- 1/4 cup pineapple juice
- 1/4 cup brown sugar
- 2 tablespoons rice vinegar
- 1 tablespoon sesame oil
- 2 cloves garlic, minced
- 1 teaspoon ginger, grated
- 1 tablespoon cornstarch (optional, for thickening)

For the Skewers:

- 1.5 to 2 pounds boneless, skinless chicken thighs, cut into bite-sized pieces
- 1 small pineapple, peeled, cored, and cut into chunks
- Bell peppers, red onions, or other vegetables of your choice, cut into chunks
- Wooden or metal skewers

Instructions:

Prepare the Marinade:
- In a bowl, whisk together soy sauce, pineapple juice, brown sugar, rice vinegar, sesame oil, minced garlic, and grated ginger. If you prefer a thicker sauce, mix in cornstarch dissolved in a little water.

Marinate the Chicken:
- Place the chicken pieces in a resealable plastic bag or a shallow dish. Pour half of the teriyaki marinade over the chicken, reserving the other half for basting and dipping. Marinate in the refrigerator for at least 30 minutes, preferably 2 hours or more.

Preheat the Grill:
- Preheat your grill or grill pan over medium-high heat.

Assemble the Skewers:
- Thread marinated chicken pieces, pineapple chunks, and vegetables onto skewers, alternating as desired.

Grill the Skewers:

- Place the skewers on the preheated grill and cook for about 10-15 minutes, turning occasionally, until the chicken is cooked through and has a nice char.

Baste with Marinade:
- Brush the skewers with the reserved teriyaki marinade during the last few minutes of grilling for added flavor.

Serve:
- Once cooked, remove the skewers from the grill and let them rest for a couple of minutes.
- Serve the teriyaki pineapple chicken skewers over rice, quinoa, or your preferred side dish.

Garnish (Optional):
- Garnish with sesame seeds, chopped green onions, or cilantro for added freshness and flavor.

Enjoy these teriyaki pineapple chicken skewers for a delightful and tropical meal with a perfect balance of sweet and savory tastes!

Rosemary Garlic Roasted Potatoes

Ingredients:

- 2 pounds baby potatoes, halved or quartered
- 3 tablespoons olive oil
- 3 cloves garlic, minced
- 1 tablespoon fresh rosemary, chopped
- 1 teaspoon dried thyme
- Salt and black pepper to taste
- Optional: Red pepper flakes for a bit of heat

Instructions:

Preheat the Oven:
- Preheat your oven to 425°F (220°C).

Prepare the Potatoes:
- Wash and cut the baby potatoes into halves or quarters, depending on their size, for uniform cooking.

Combine Ingredients:
- In a large bowl, combine the halved potatoes with olive oil, minced garlic, chopped fresh rosemary, dried thyme, salt, black pepper, and red pepper flakes (if using). Toss until the potatoes are well coated.

Arrange on Baking Sheet:
- Spread the seasoned potatoes in a single layer on a baking sheet lined with parchment paper. Ensure that the potatoes are not overcrowded to allow for even roasting.

Roast in the Oven:
- Roast the potatoes in the preheated oven for 25-30 minutes or until they are golden brown and crispy on the edges. Stir the potatoes halfway through the cooking time for even browning.

Check for Doneness:
- Test the potatoes with a fork to ensure they are tender on the inside.

Serve:
- Once roasted to perfection, remove the potatoes from the oven and transfer them to a serving dish.

Garnish (Optional):
- Garnish with additional fresh rosemary or thyme if desired.

These rosemary garlic roasted potatoes make a delicious side dish for any meal. They are versatile, easy to prepare, and bring a wonderful aroma and flavor to your table. Enjoy!

Air Fryer Ratatouille

Ingredients:

- 1 eggplant, diced
- 1 zucchini, diced
- 1 yellow squash, diced
- 1 bell pepper (any color), diced
- 1 red onion, diced
- 2 tomatoes, diced
- 3 cloves garlic, minced
- 2 tablespoons olive oil
- 1 teaspoon dried thyme
- 1 teaspoon dried rosemary
- Salt and black pepper to taste
- 1/4 cup fresh basil, chopped (for garnish)
- Grated Parmesan cheese (optional, for serving)

Instructions:

Preheat the Air Fryer:
- Preheat your air fryer to 375°F (190°C).

Prepare the Vegetables:
- In a large bowl, combine the diced eggplant, zucchini, yellow squash, bell pepper, red onion, tomatoes, and minced garlic.

Season:
- Drizzle olive oil over the vegetables and sprinkle with dried thyme, dried rosemary, salt, and black pepper. Toss the vegetables until evenly coated with the seasonings.

Air Fry:
- Place the seasoned vegetables in the air fryer basket in a single layer. You may need to cook them in batches depending on the size of your air fryer.

Cook in Batches:
- Air fry the vegetables for 15-20 minutes, shaking the basket or stirring halfway through the cooking time. Cook until the vegetables are tender and slightly caramelized.

Garnish and Serve:
- Once done, transfer the air-fried ratatouille to a serving dish. Garnish with fresh chopped basil and, if desired, sprinkle with grated Parmesan cheese before serving.

Optional: Baking Variation
- Alternatively, you can spread the seasoned vegetables on a baking sheet and roast them in a preheated oven at 375°F (190°C) for 25-30 minutes, stirring halfway through.

This air fryer ratatouille is a flavorful and vibrant dish that makes a great side or even a light vegetarian main course. Enjoy the rich taste of roasted vegetables with the convenience of your air fryer!

Chocolate Chip Banana Bread Muffins

Ingredients:

- 3 ripe bananas, mashed
- 1/2 cup unsalted butter, melted
- 1 teaspoon vanilla extract
- 1 egg
- 1/2 cup granulated sugar
- 1/4 cup brown sugar, packed
- 1 1/2 cups all-purpose flour
- 1 teaspoon baking powder
- 1/2 teaspoon baking soda
- 1/4 teaspoon salt
- 1 cup chocolate chips
- Optional: Chopped nuts (such as walnuts or pecans)

Instructions:

Preheat the Oven:
- Preheat your oven to 350°F (175°C). Line a muffin tin with paper liners or grease the muffin cups.

Mash Bananas:
- In a large mixing bowl, mash the ripe bananas with a fork or potato masher.

Combine Wet Ingredients:
- Add melted butter, vanilla extract, egg, granulated sugar, and brown sugar to the mashed bananas. Mix until well combined.

Combine Dry Ingredients:
- In a separate bowl, whisk together the flour, baking powder, baking soda, and salt.

Combine Wet and Dry Ingredients:
- Gradually add the dry ingredients to the wet ingredients, stirring until just combined. Be careful not to overmix.

Fold in Chocolate Chips:
- Gently fold in the chocolate chips and, if desired, chopped nuts.

Fill Muffin Cups:
- Spoon the batter into the prepared muffin cups, filling each about 2/3 to 3/4 full.

Bake:

- Bake in the preheated oven for 18-20 minutes or until a toothpick inserted into the center of a muffin comes out clean or with a few moist crumbs.

Cool:
- Allow the muffins to cool in the tin for a few minutes before transferring them to a wire rack to cool completely.

Serve:
- Once cooled, enjoy these delicious chocolate chip banana bread muffins!

These muffins are a perfect treat for breakfast or as a snack. The combination of ripe bananas and chocolate chips creates a moist and flavorful treat that's sure to be a hit!

Pecan-Crusted Air Fryer Chicken Tenders

Ingredients:

For the Pecan Coating:

- 1 cup pecans, finely chopped
- 1/2 cup breadcrumbs
- 1 teaspoon dried thyme
- 1 teaspoon garlic powder
- 1/2 teaspoon paprika
- Salt and black pepper to taste

For the Chicken:

- 1.5 to 2 pounds chicken tenders
- 2 eggs, beaten
- Cooking spray

Instructions:

Preheat the Air Fryer:
- Preheat your air fryer to 400°F (200°C).

Prepare Pecan Coating:
- In a shallow bowl, combine finely chopped pecans, breadcrumbs, dried thyme, garlic powder, paprika, salt, and black pepper. Mix well.

Coat the Chicken:
- Dip each chicken tender into the beaten eggs, ensuring it's well coated.

Coat with Pecan Mixture:
- Press the egg-coated chicken tender into the pecan mixture, ensuring the pecans adhere to the chicken. Coat both sides evenly.

Place on Air Fryer Basket:
- Place the coated chicken tenders in the air fryer basket in a single layer. You may need to cook them in batches to avoid overcrowding.

Spray with Cooking Spray:
- Lightly spray the coated chicken tenders with cooking spray. This helps them crisp up in the air fryer.

Air Fry:
- Air fry at 400°F (200°C) for 12-15 minutes, flipping the tenders halfway through the cooking time. Cook until the chicken is golden brown and cooked through.

Check for Doneness:
- Ensure that the internal temperature of the chicken reaches 165°F (74°C).

Serve:
- Once done, remove the pecan-crusted chicken tenders from the air fryer and let them rest for a few minutes.

Optional Dip:
- Serve with your favorite dipping sauce, such as honey mustard or ranch.

Enjoy these pecan-crusted air fryer chicken tenders as a tasty and healthier alternative to traditional fried chicken tenders. They're perfect for a quick and flavorful meal!

Lemon Herb Roasted Asparagus

Ingredients:

- 1 bunch fresh asparagus, tough ends trimmed
- 2 tablespoons olive oil
- Zest of 1 lemon
- 2 tablespoons fresh lemon juice
- 2 cloves garlic, minced
- 1 teaspoon dried thyme (or 1 tablespoon fresh thyme, chopped)
- Salt and black pepper to taste
- Optional: Grated Parmesan cheese for serving

Instructions:

Preheat the Oven:
- Preheat your oven to 400°F (200°C).

Prepare the Asparagus:
- Trim the tough ends of the asparagus spears. If they are thick, you can peel the bottom half with a vegetable peeler for a more tender result.

Arrange on Baking Sheet:
- Place the trimmed asparagus on a baking sheet in a single layer.

Prepare the Marinade:
- In a small bowl, whisk together olive oil, lemon zest, lemon juice, minced garlic, dried thyme, salt, and black pepper.

Coat the Asparagus:
- Drizzle the lemon herb marinade over the asparagus, tossing to coat evenly. Ensure each spear is well coated.

Roast in the Oven:
- Roast in the preheated oven for 12-15 minutes or until the asparagus is tender but still crisp.

Optional Broil:
- If you prefer a bit of char on the asparagus, you can broil for an additional 1-2 minutes, watching closely to prevent burning.

Serve:
- Transfer the roasted asparagus to a serving dish. Optionally, sprinkle with grated Parmesan cheese before serving.

Enjoy this lemon herb roasted asparagus as a vibrant and flavorful side dish that adds a burst of freshness to your meal. It's a perfect accompaniment to a variety of dishes, from roasted chicken to grilled fish.

Air Fryer Beef and Vegetable Kebabs

Ingredients:

For the Marinade:

- 1.5 pounds beef sirloin or your preferred cut, cut into bite-sized cubes
- 1/4 cup soy sauce
- 2 tablespoons olive oil
- 2 tablespoons Worcestershire sauce
- 2 cloves garlic, minced
- 1 teaspoon Dijon mustard
- 1 teaspoon smoked paprika
- 1 teaspoon dried oregano
- 1/2 teaspoon black pepper

For the Kebabs:

- Bell peppers, cut into chunks (assorted colors)
- Cherry tomatoes
- Red onion, cut into chunks
- Mushrooms, whole or halved
- Wooden or metal skewers

Instructions:

Prepare the Marinade:
- In a bowl, whisk together soy sauce, olive oil, Worcestershire sauce, minced garlic, Dijon mustard, smoked paprika, dried oregano, and black pepper.

Marinate the Beef:
- Place the beef cubes in a resealable plastic bag or a shallow dish. Pour the marinade over the beef, ensuring it's well coated. Marinate for at least 30 minutes, or ideally, refrigerate for 2-4 hours for maximum flavor.

Preheat the Air Fryer:
- Preheat your air fryer to 400°F (200°C).

Assemble the Kebabs:
- Thread the marinated beef cubes, bell pepper chunks, cherry tomatoes, red onion chunks, and mushrooms onto the skewers, alternating the ingredients.

Air Fry:

- Place the assembled kebabs in the air fryer basket in a single layer, leaving space between them for even cooking.

Air Fry the Kebabs:
- Air fry at 400°F (200°C) for 10-12 minutes, turning the kebabs halfway through the cooking time. Cook until the beef reaches your desired level of doneness and the vegetables are tender and slightly charred.

Serve:
- Once done, transfer the beef and vegetable kebabs to a serving platter.

Garnish (Optional):
- Garnish with fresh herbs like parsley or cilantro before serving.

Enjoy these flavorful and juicy air fryer beef and vegetable kebabs as a satisfying and healthy meal. Serve them with your favorite side dishes or a bed of rice for a complete and delicious dinner!

www.ingramcontent.com/pod-product-compliance
Lightning Source LLC
LaVergne TN
LVHW081603060526
838201LV00054B/2055